Hello French!

Colour In

French

la cheminée
la sheh-mee-neh *chimney*

le toit
ler twah *roof*

la fenêtre
la f'net-tr' *window*

la clôture
la klot-yoor *fence*

l'échelle
leh-shel *ladder*

la porte
la port *door*

la poubelle
la poo-bel *bin*

le tuyau d'arrosage
ler twee-yo da-roh-saj *hose pipe*

l'herbe
lairb *grass*

À la plage

ah la plash   At the beach

le ciel
ler see-el *sky*

le sable
ler sabl' *sand*

le parasol
ler parasol *beach umbrella*

la planche de surf
la pla(n)-sh der surf
surfboard

la crème solaire
la krem sol-air *sun cream*

le coquillage
ler kok-ee-ash *seashell*

la pelle
la pel *spade*

le seau
ler sew *bucket*

le phare
ler far *lighthouse*

la mouette
la moo-et *seagull*

la vague
la vah-g *wave*

le bateau
ler bat-o *boat*

les algues
leh zalg' *seaweed*

le rocher
ler rosheh *rock*

le château de sable
ler shat-o der sabl' *sand castle*

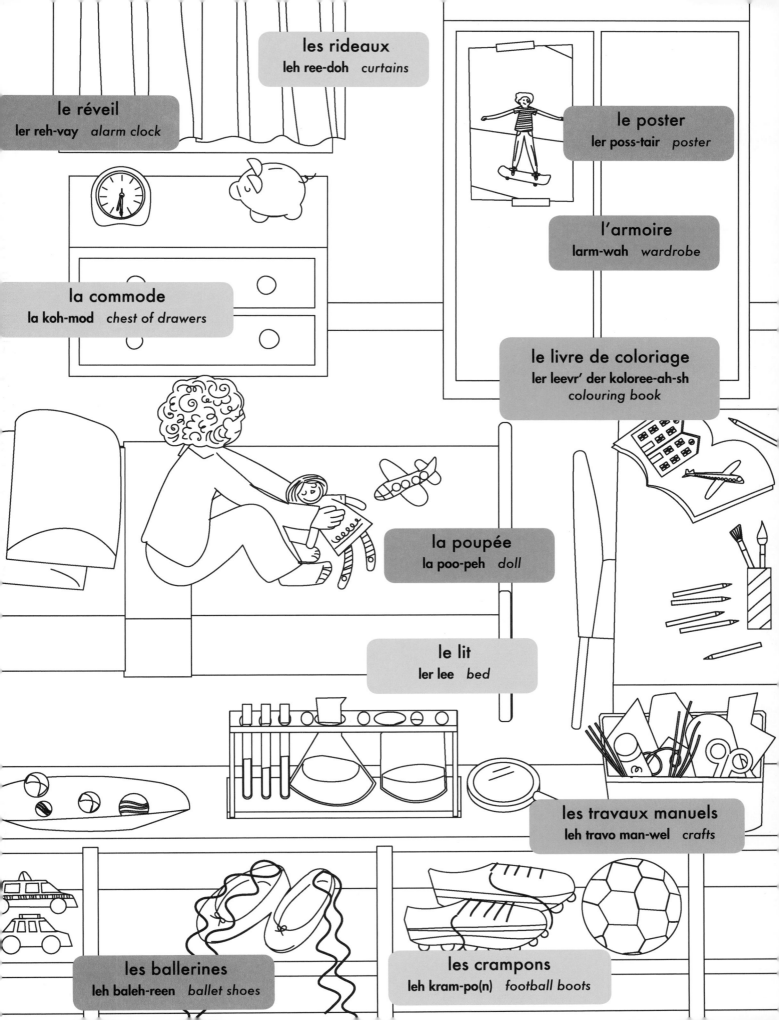

les rideaux
leh ree-doh curtains

le réveil
ler reh-vay alarm clock

le poster
ler poss-tair poster

l'armoire
larm-wah wardrobe

la commode
la koh-mod chest of drawers

le livre de coloriage
ler leevr' der koloree-ah-sh
colouring book

la poupée
la poo-peh doll

le lit
ler lee bed

les travaux manuels
leh travo man-wel crafts

les ballerines
leh baleh-reen ballet shoes

les crampons
leh kram-po(n) football boots

le champ
ler sho(n) *field*

la grange
la gronsh *barn*

le cheval
ler sh'val *horse*

le poulain
ler pool-a(n) *foal*

le cochon
ler koh-sho(n) *pig*

la fermière
la fairm-ee-err *farmer (woman)*

le lapin
ler lapa(n) *rabbit*

le porcelet
ler por-ser-leh *piglet*

le chat
ler chah *cat*

la chèvre
la shevr' *goat*

la souris
la syoo-ree *mouse*

Jouer
shoo-eh   *Playing*

grimper
grampeh   *climbing*

cacher
kasheh   *hiding*

sauter à la corde
so-teh ah la kord
skipping

pousser
poosseh   *pushing*

courir
koor-eer   *running*

serrer dans ses bras
serreh do(n) seh brah   *hugging*

porter
por-teh   *carrying*

marcher
marsheh   *walking*

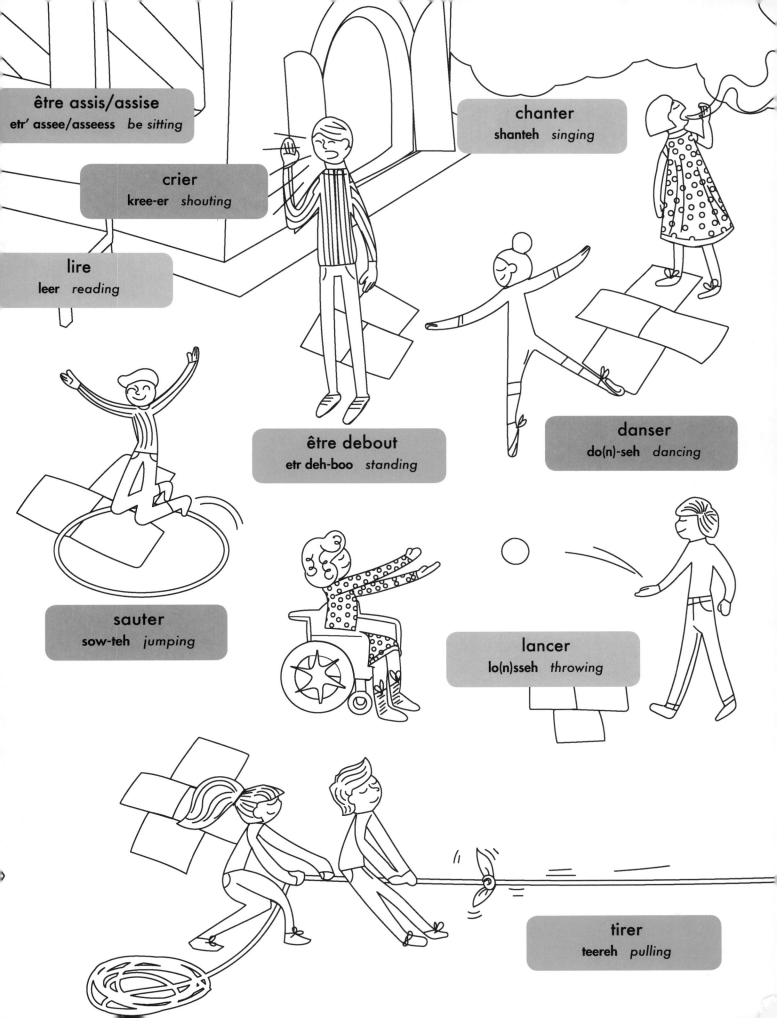

être assis/assise
etr' assee/asseess *be sitting*

crier
kree-er *shouting*

lire
leer *reading*

chanter
shanteh *singing*

danser
do(n)-seh *dancing*

être debout
etr deh-boo *standing*

sauter
sow-teh *jumping*

lancer
lo(n)sseh *throwing*

tirer
teereh *pulling*

À la bibliothèque

ah la beeblee-oh-tek

At the library

les histoires
lez eestwaar *stories*

l'étagère
letasher *shelf*

la bande dessinée
la bond dess-ee-neh
comic

le pirate
ler peerat *pirate*

la sorcière
la sorsee-air *witch*

la fée
la feh *fairy*

la licorne
la leekorn *unicorn*

la sirène
la see-ren *mermaid*

le chevalier
ler sher-valee-yeh *knight*

la princesse
la pra(n)-sess *princess*

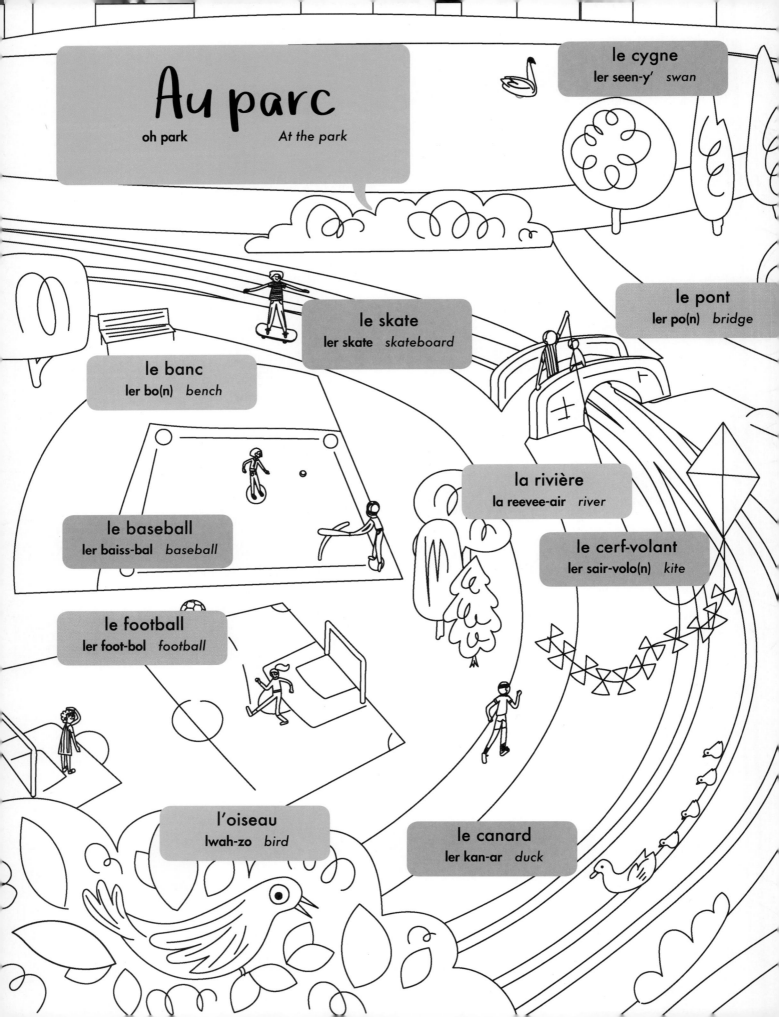

le basket
ler bass-ket basketball

le tennis
ler ten-eess tennis

la gymnastique
la sheem-nass-teek
gymnastics

le vélo
ler vailo bicycle

le rugby
ler roog-bee rugby

la glace
la glas ice cream

l'écureuil
leh-kooray squirrel

le chien
ler shee-ya(n) dog

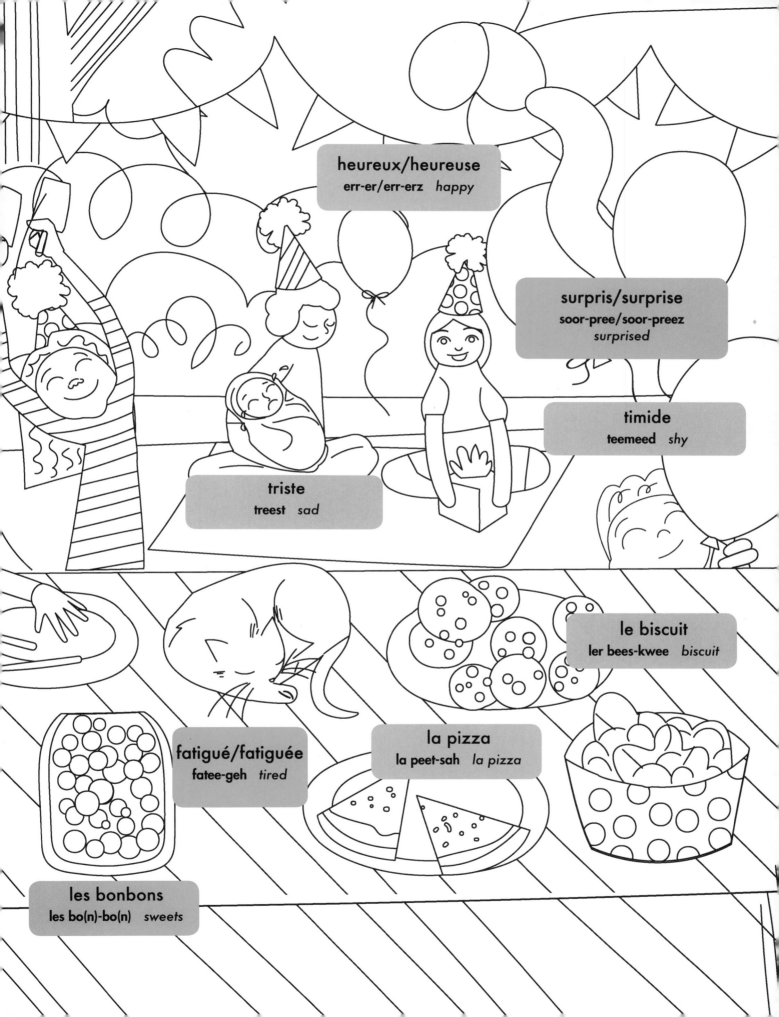

heureux/heureuse
err-er/err-erz *happy*

surpris/surprise
soor-pree/soor-preez
surprised

timide
teemeed *shy*

triste
treest *sad*

le biscuit
ler bees-kwee *biscuit*

fatigué/fatiguée
fatee-geh *tired*

la pizza
la peet-sah *la pizza*

les bonbons
les bo(n)-bo(n) *sweets*

À l'école

ah lekol   *At school*

le tableau blanc
ler tab-loh blo(n)   *whiteboard*

le calendrier
ler kalon-dree-yeh   *calendar*

l'alphabet
lalfabeh   *alphabet*

le maître
ler metr'   *teacher (man)*

le stylo
ler steelo   *pen*

la colle
la kol   *glue*

les ciseaux
leh seezo   *scissors*

la chaise
la shez   *chair*

la maîtresse
la met-ress *teacher (woman)*

la pendule
la pond-yule *clock*

le livre
ler leevr' *book*

le bureau
ler b-yooro *desk*

le papier
ler pap-ee-eh *paper*

la peinture
la pant-yoor *paints*

le crayon de couleur
ler krayo(n) der kool-err *colouring pencil*

le shampooing
ler shom-poo-a(n)   *shampoo*

les lunettes de natation
leh loo-net der natassee-yo(n)
swimming goggles

le maillot de bain
er my-yo der ba(n)   *swimming costume*

le bonnet de bain
ler bonneh der ba(n)   *swimming cap*

le cours de natation
ler koor der natassee-yo(n)
swimming lesson

les brassards
leh brass-ar   *armbands*

la natation
la natassee-yo(n)   *swimming*

la piscine
la pee-seen   *swimming pool*

En ville

on veel   *In town*

le train
ler tra(n)   *train*

la poste
la post   *post office*

le camion de pompiers
ler kamee-o(n) der pomp-ee-eh
fire engine

la voiture
la vwat-yoor   *car*

la moto
la moh-toh   *motorbike*

le taxi
ler tax-ee   *taxi*

la voiture de police
la vwat-yoor der poleess   *police car*

l'avion
lavee-o(n) *aeroplane*

la gare
la gaar *train station*

le cinéma
ler seenem-a *cinema*

le parking
ler parkeeng *car park*

l'hôpital
lopee-tal *hospital*

la mairie
la mair-ree *town hall*

l'ambulance
lamboo-lonss *ambulance*

le bus
ler booss *bus*

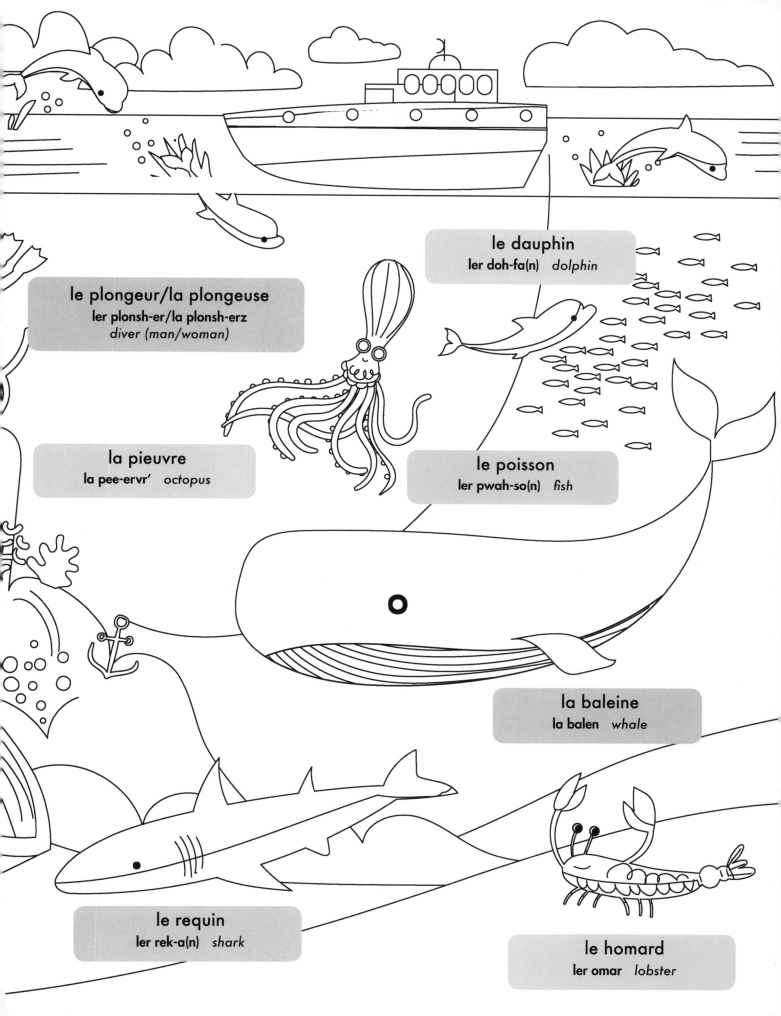

le dauphin
ler doh-fa(n) *dolphin*

le plongeur/la plongeuse
ler plonsh-er/la plonsh-erz
diver (man/woman)

la pieuvre
la pee-ervr' *octopus*

le poisson
ler pwah-so(n) *fish*

la baleine
la balen *whale*

le requin
ler rek-a(n) *shark*

le homard
ler omar *lobster*

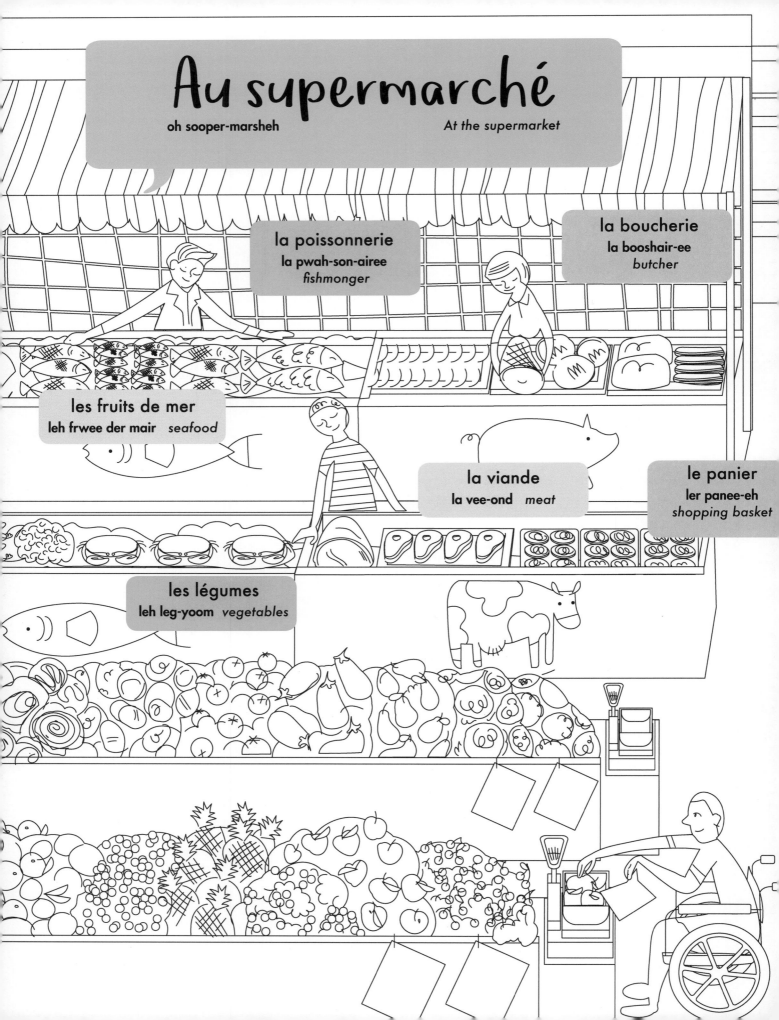

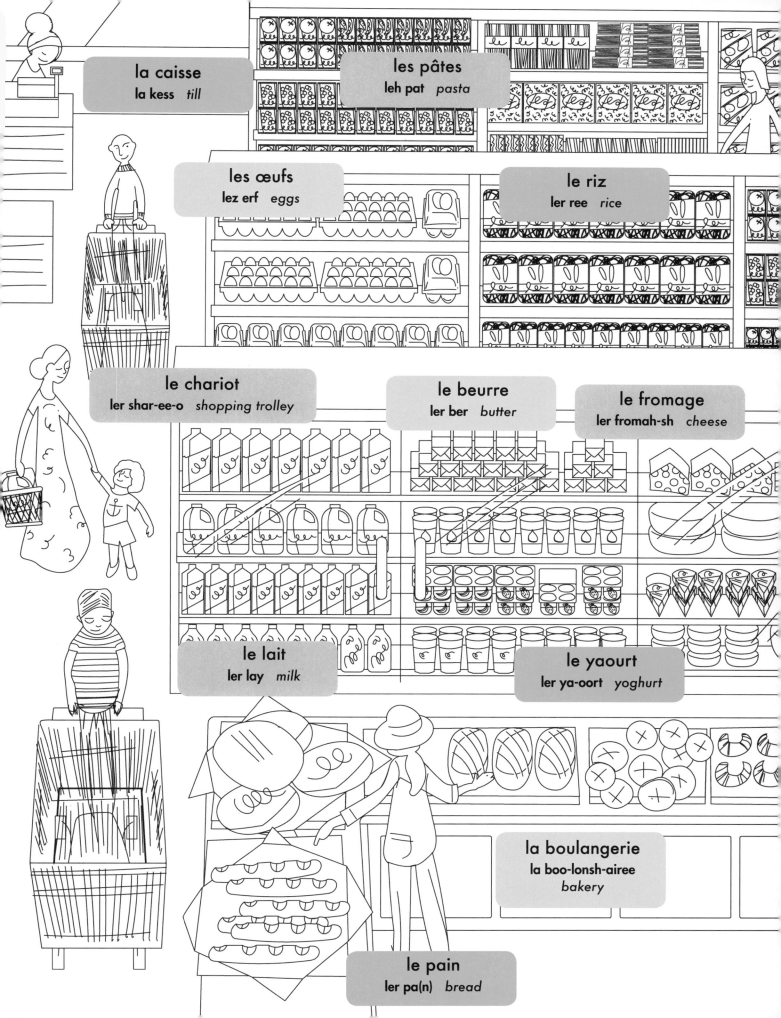

la caisse
la kess *till*

les pâtes
leh pat *pasta*

les œufs
lez erf *eggs*

le riz
ler ree *rice*

le chariot
ler shar-ee-o *shopping trolley*

le beurre
ler ber *butter*

le fromage
ler fromah-sh *cheese*

le lait
ler lay *milk*

le yaourt
ler ya-oort *yoghurt*

la boulangerie
la boo-lonsh-airee
bakery

le pain
ler pa(n) *bread*

l'escalier
less-kalee-eh *stairs*

le téléphone
ler teh-leh-fon *telephone*

le canapé
ler kanap-eh *sofa*

le coussin
ler kooss-a(n) *cushion*

la télévision
la teh-leh-veezee-o(n) *television*

la tasse de thé
la tass der teh *cup of tea*

le café
ler kaf-eh *coffee*

le fauteuil
ler fo-tuh-yee *armchair*

written by Sam Hutchinson & Emilie Martin

illustrated by Kim Hankinson

French adviser: Marie-Thérèse Bougard

Published by b small publishing ltd.

www.bsmall.co.uk

Text & Illustrations copyright © b small publishing ltd. 2018

2 3 4 5

ISBN 978-1-911509-79-0

Design: Kim Hankinson   Editorial: Emilie Martin & Rachel Thorpe   Production: Madeleine Ehm

Publisher: Sam Hutchinson

Printed in China by WKT Co. Ltd.